Unity for What?

Unity for What?

Carter M. Head

Heads Up Publications

Atlanta

All rights reserved. No part of this book may be reproduced or transmitted in any form or by any means, electronic or mechanical, including photocopying, recording or any information storage and retrieval system without written permission of the author except for brief quotations used in reviews, written specifically for inclusion in a newspaper, blog, magazine, or academic paper.

Scripture quotations marked (KJV) are from the King James Version of the Bible.

Unity for What?
Copyright © 2018 by Carter M. Head
Published by Heads Up Publications
Editor: Lashuntay Wilson
Cover by Pierre McCummings

ISBN: 978-0-9988323-3-3
Ebook ISBN: 978-0-9988323-6-4
Library of Congress Control Number: 2018946749

Heads Up Publications Books are available at special discounts for bulk purchases for sales or premiums.
Direct all inquiries and correspondence to:
Heads Up Publications
P.O Box 162593
Atlanta, GA 30321
e-mail: headsuppublications@gmail.com

Printed in the United States of America

THIS BOOK IS DEDICATED TO:

SEMETRICE DILWORTH

CARLOUS MCKIBBEN HEAD

YVETTE HEAD

MARCOUS HEAD

CHINA HEAD - OLIPHANT

ALEX HAWKINS

Contents

Introduction………………IX

CHAPTER 1
Unity versus Diversity……………..,,,*15*

CHAPTER 2
Uniformity is Not the Key……………*23*

CHAPTER 3
Tribalism…………………………….*27*

CHAPTER 4
The 3-D Effect of Unity ………………*33*

CHAPTER 5
Eradicating Divisions…………………*39*

CHAPTER 6
Why Don't We Like Each Other?..........*47*

CHAPTER 7
Unity Misconceived……......................*51*

CHAPTER 8
Peace on Earth……………….……...*55*

Introduction

Many people are not for unity forming because some of them do not want to be servants or slaves to someone else, they rather be served. What I have found before writing this compendium, is that uniformity does not always mean alignment and agreeing on all points of its conceptualized views. What I want to share in this book, is that unity is obviously about diversity, different from uniformity which is about similarity in concepts. Unity is only an intricate part of a unit with an ultimate goal and this book shows that goal. Which is for the peaceful fulfillment and collective prosperity in health and finances for all of humanity.

Just about everyone is affiliated with their particular group or organization with the same mindsets as they, but each member sometimes having different outlooks on life in reference to humanity as a whole and that's okay. It's about time for the human race to be ok with diversity and differences amongst our fellow humans and be respectful and humbled because of all the vast, distinctive degrees of unconformity in our existences in the God created worlds. Because God did create the worlds and God created differences in the world. For those of you that believe in God the creator and those of you that do not; we all must find a common paradigm with the fact that something or someone of substance started this world. With that stated; in this compendium, I will come from the premise of God obviously creating differences in languages mindsets, colors, shapes, sizes and ideas of all individuals in our human race.

Now for those of us that have read and researched the biblical text; being that most of us intellectual and inquiring minded people who are readers, surely by now read in the book of Genesis chapter 11 verse 1-9, we find where it is written that the whole earth was united, the people in that time was of one language and of one speech. They all had traveled together and found a place to build a city and a tower whose top may reach unto the heavens. This people also made one name unto themselves in order not be scattered abroad upon the face of the whole earth. When God saw and said; these people are unified and have one language and whatever they imagine doing will be done without restraint. So, God confused the people language so each of them would not understand one another's speech. This biblical writing shared that God scattered them abroad throughout the face of all the earth and the people cease from building the tower that they were unified in building.

Since then; the question was posed and even today many are still asking the question. Why did God divide a unified people that were obviously on one accord in total agreement? Well I decided to write a book in reference to my insight and research about this dilemma in which division are a major component in our human existence and experiences even with other people throughout this world. Before reading this book ask yourself has unifying worked for

Humanity as a whole in all areas of life from a positive, productive and compassionate parameter or have most unified organizations depleted and denounced the mere camaraderie of some not affiliated with their particular groups…

1

Unity Verses Diversity

Unity is usually exclusiveness which limits to possession, control, or use by a single individual or group, excluding others from participation. The emphasis on grouping or unifying confines our society to mere labels. We should not have to be conformed by one label, we can be liberated as an intricate part of humanity as a whole. We have to address the mental stability and prowess of the people we are trying to or considering unifying with. Most people only stand and agree in unison when it is convenient and conducive for their individual situation and concepts. There is always before us when dealing with and attempting to unify with others, the term called cognitive dissonance; which means the mental discomfort experienced by a person who simultaneously holds two or more contradictory beliefs, ideas or values thus making them double minded or confused. How do we expect to unify with potentially disoriented people when all of us at some point have disagreements

Unity should go beyond the structure of specific groups, sect, fashion, tribe, clan and organization. Especially in areas of expressed common ground in order to solidify persons understanding of promoting a humanitarian construct in reference to helping all humans indirectly and directly. We can be diverse by showing a great deal or variety by various forms of ideas and insight in reference to a specific topic and situations dealing with all humans on a positive conclusion, but diversity hurts all involved when it is directed towards dividing in order to destroy, discredit and to others demise.

Consider this when attempting to devise ways to eradicate racism throughout the world, realizing what actually happens in the construct of unifying and uniting. Most groups have a strong influence on a certain person because of the particular person culture or upbringing by the subliminals presented to the person eyes and ears causing that individual to be more excited and susceptible to the influence of familiarity about a certain subject and topic. Most humans are so intrigued with knowledge and truth until we quickly receive new information as truth in relations to any said topic of our familiarity, thus making it doctrine and then begin to indoctrinate others with same information. But I humbly submit to you that if any information that each of us humans receive and perceive is truth, should not only be truth to our designated group only, but that truth should essentially be used to emphasize basic fundamental or intrinsic nature and the wellbeing of all humans and Humanity.

    Be mindful and careful when your sole purpose and mission is to only help and advance the people affiliated with your group. That is not the true unity of humanity. That is unity that secretly and sometimes unknowingly divides. Be reminded, we all, no matter what group we claim affiliation with, find out the common cause and motivation of that particular group express a mentality of having a heart to help all people, protection of all humans and the prosperity or well being of all humanity and nature. This is very possible. It may not be your group total intent but there should be certain measures implemented in your groups doctrine and belief systems that will allow opportunities for you all to at least discuss ways to unite with all humans. For example: when the Olympic game occur, the starting ceremony influence all nationalities in the arena to stand and applaud together and at the same time even for other nationalities.

This effort is the same in sports where both opposing teams stand together when the anthem is played. Collectively we humans can sometimes find ways to unify on commonly associated areas of our lives as humans.

We must consider sharing in a group setting or construct, by expressing your ideas and prospectives openly, putting forth an effort in being persistent in sharing information and your objective beliefs also may allow all others to express their difference of opinions and belief without harm, ostracization, belittlement and even death because of opposition. Everyone may not agree with certain groups beliefs, traditions and laws, but we all must learn to respect one another views without oppressing them because of their different views. Again, when we all consider this, maybe we all, no matter what group we come from, will try to come to a common sensible state of humbleness in order to unify more in reference to humanity as a whole.

2

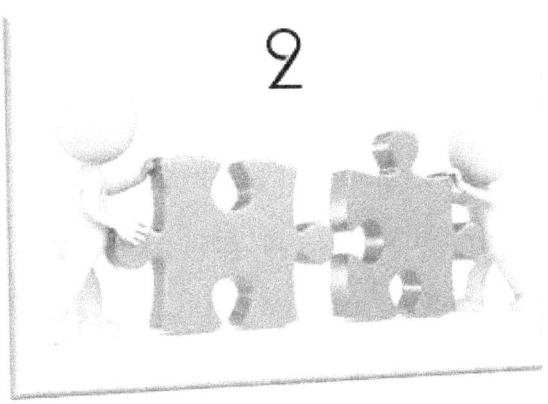

Uniformity is Not the Key

Uniformity is over all sameness, homogeneity, regularity, and unity of style and agreement with one another in a particular area is good ethics and morals when what is being agreed upon is for the good of all. Agreement amongst a group of people who has selfless and grievous intentions is wrong. But we all must admit that agreement promotes and solidifies a certain level of intrinsic power and this can become why destruction towards other groups of people with different concepts and prospective are an intricate part of the groups mentality and motives.

Let's look at uniformity as being a good conception reference to our armed forces, that consist of the Navy, Marines, Army, Airforce and there are even more special services coming from these sections the United States Armed Forces. The question has been asked of some of these service men and women; should all armed forces be unified in rank? Seventy six percent that were asked, said no and 4 percent said it does not matter. The reason most of them that were surveyed said no was because combining to one would take away the heritage of the branch of service. I concur, sometimes unifying as one takes away broader and various perspectives that could possibly enhance more help towards and in humanity as a whole, one entity can ever do what multitudes can do. This is why we as a people must reconsider or reevaluate why most of us are locked into the following only one organizations ideology and concept; that all the time denounce, belittles, cast aside and discredits other organizations, promulgating them and their organization to be the only rational entity. This notice limits humanity as a whole and the human continuity and other creative mindsets. We must resist "One person or one group concepts" as being the ultimate way. Uniformity in this effort does not help humanity as a whole in reference to expanding in all areas of this life, and the progression of human existence and is not the key to sustain productive human existence confirmed with peace assurance and advancement.

3

Tribalism

No more tribalism, clans, sects, or groups. The concept of united groups limits us all because this ideology is the behavior and attitudes that stem from strong loyalty to one's own tribe, social or political group. Being organized as an advocate for that specific group and do not for the whole human race.

Different and multiple ideas bring more creations. Single ideas bring about less creations and one concept brings about followers of that one ideology in which develops a cult, a clan, a group and tribalism making it all about one-person mindset, this is what limits us. All humans can contribute not just only a few charismatic people. We all are one piece of the puzzle. Tribalism discourages connecting with other groups outside of their sect.

Most of our lives all of us have been hearing statements made about people getting together and unifying. But when the concept of unity is promulgated wrongfully, it contributes to separatist propaganda with the mission and motive to divide and discredit.

This is the secret weapon that has infiltrated our world view point for centuries and unknowingly we all have contributed to the cause of negativity unifying in an effort to oppose, disapprove, disassociate with other groups and other humans.

Many groups of people have united in order to start conquests and overturn or conquer, I call it the great divider. Let's address four groups and their intentions. We have what is called Nationality; which is the status of belonging to a particular nation and is bias towards other nationalities. Then we have Nations, which unite but common descent, history, culture, or language inhabiting a particular country or territory with different views of other nations. There is also Dynasties that are a line of hereditary rulers of a country that disregards any other person that is not in agreement with their rule. Then there are Empires which are an extensive group of states or countries under a single supreme authority like an emperor who opposes anyone that opposes their structure. All of these are what I call separation separatist the promulgate and instill fear and suspicions towards and about others that are not part of their group.

We must understand and acknowledge our beliefs sometimes keeps us separated even when we think it is for a good cause. For this I say unity is misconceived and misused for negative agendas. Allow me to be very clear, I am not expressing that you, I or anyone should not be a part of a family structure or group setting. I am not saying that we should not associate with others on specific issues, values, ideas and beliefs. But I believe no group or organization should have to believe that any one group supersedes the rights of another group even when each of their views are opposite in ideologies, structures and beliefs. All of our groups should influence the fulfillment and progression in worldwide peace and prosperity for the entire human race as a whole, not for destruction and demise. Just know what unifying means to me is a state of oneness, being unified as a whole with one conceived agenda; that is all people having success in this world, even subconsciously with our thoughts in reference the propriety of humanity and nature.

4

The 3-D Effect of Unity

True uniformity is what I call the three–dimensional effect that is derived of the concept from our physical environment which is 3-D and we humans move around in this three – dimensional construct every day. It is the width, height and depth of our appearance and what we display. The movie producers use this to design and produce 3-D movies with the motive of giving the viewers a visual imagery that stands out beyond the screen. Well though this compendium will attempt to promulgate a similar effect and illustration of unity by this same 3-D construct that we all are already experiencing on a daily basis, but maybe not aware of as of yet.

Here it is; we tend to unify with our desired and chosen groups by mere acknowledgement of an agreed doctrine or viewpoint, which is one dimensional. It only satisfies a certain but single-minded motive that satisfies that particular group or organization. But a three-dimensional mindset and motive express at least three different approaches when considering with others in order to unify, which are:

A. A purpose that will benefit humanity as a whole.
B. A concept that will bring peace within that is expressed outwardly towards all other humans
C. Collaborating with others of different characteristics, but the same ultimate goals that will not ostracize any other human.

When we all can initiate these traits and understanding only then will we operate from a three-dimensional construct in the efforts of uniting all of the human race. I know this sounds farfetched, but it is not impossible to those of us that are willing participants for the cause of unifying for only our preferred groups.

I am hopeful that there are many more amongst us that unknowingly are our confidants and constituents that after reading this book will then begin a quest in connect for all the reasons in reference to advancing relations in the whole of humanity. Again, this three-dimensional concept I am promulgating is the depth of the reasoning of you bringing in unity with a group, which is the effort to broaden your mentality of your acceptance of others. The height of your consciousness that will lead to you seeing from a whole different level of precepting opposite of the way you have viewed others from different groups. Also, the extension of your belief system you have been in indoctrinated with throughout your life thus far. By gaining more knowledge, more truth, more awareness, more love towards all others and more deliverance from divisive mindsets towards others. In which determines the length of a sincere hearted person with a motive to celebrate with others outside our groups for greater purposes towards all of humanity.

5

Eradicating Divisions

We have all heard of suggestions on stopping divisions. Allow me to be clear, there are two types of divisions: Divisive Divisions and Progressive Divisions. Divisive Divisions tend to cause disagreement or hostility between people, it alienates, estrange, isolate and set its rivals against each other. Progressive Divisions advocate progress, change, improvement, and reform, as opposed to wanting to keep things as they are especially in political and religious matters.

So, in order to eradicate divisions, we must understand the difference of the two types of divisions and put forth a conscious effort to determine a good divide from a bad divider. Be reminded a good divider will progress and evolve in a valid means of making things better for the whole of humanity eventually if and only when we all do our part as individuals and have the mindset and compassion to be prompt at all time to know we choose to be apart of any group and at least listen to any group that motives are to help assist other groups in an effort to unite Humanity in love, peace and assurance in the common cause of expanding hope and tranquility in this world for all humans.

You may ask; Do I think this is possible or do I believe unifying all humans will happen. My answer to you is; I am always optimistic and hopeful, but it is very unlikely. But that is not to say, we should all not put forth an individual valiant effort to pull down bad and negative divisive divisions and support ideas of a united concept of respect and honor for the diverse group of people who ideals are governed by inventing and constructing ways to help humanity as whole. Not just helping their own groups. **Hate groups** have beliefs and practices that attack or malign an entire class of people, typically for their immutable characteristics.

Hate groups have grew by 197 percent since 2015. There are an estimate 920 hate groups Religious groups are estimated at roughly 4,200 different groups in the world.

Religious groups operate with faith or belief systems. Religion differs from private belief in that it has a public aspect but, in most cases, not the outlook at acceptance of all humans.

Political groups there are nearly 50 political parties in the United States many of which are active and regularly offer a candidate for president but only mostly dominated by a two-party system. Political parties are organized groups of people with at least roughly similar political aim and opinions that seeks to influence public policy. Neither of these political parties exemplify the concept of one race; the human race as being the ultimate goal as of implementing equality for humanity and every human throughout the world they all make emphasis on equality without any measures or proof to the effect of policies actually being put in place for it to happen.

Ethnic groups are a community or population made up of people who share a common cultural background or descent. Each group believing, they are opposite of all other groups. There are anyway from 23,000 to 24,000 different ethic groups in the world. Listen we are different in a lot of ways. Yet I believe we the human race possess the ability deep within each of our personalities to not only exist on this plant together but also to exist in harmony.

Social groups are defined as two or more people who interact with one another, share similar characteristics and collectively have a sense of unity. But usually unify and bond amongst their confines and circles of interest. Most of these group discriminate and oppose other groups.

So, allow me to ask you are there any united groups in this world that propagate unity, love, peace, hope, assurance and well being for all humans, the prosperous and fulfilled livelihood of humanity, without reserve and bias? If your answer is no, we must collectively agree that unifying does not work as to the construct of our format or structured organized concept of unity. But there is a solid solution. Let's begin within ourselves and start by desiring a better way for all humanity and possibly we can eradicate divisions.

6

Why Don't We Like Each Other

More often than none most humans only like people who like us, we tend to appreciate people of similar mindsets, upbringing, religion beliefs, social status and same ethnicity as ours. When others do not look like, dress like, conform to or connect with our sense of being most tend to reject, object to and cast aside in reference to those and many more differences a person may have. Which causes some people to group up against others that have chosen to group up. We have allowed this mindset to even exist in the fun games and sport we enjoy, in which puts us at opposition with the opposing team and player. It brings into play the competitiveness within our soul, that is being groomed every day through media, coach's, parents and associates, impressing on our thoughts to be better than others and think towards others as being the lessor and the enemy. This further divide us as people as a people as humans.

    We must begin to respect, honor and expect the fact that all of us are different in a lot of values, concepts, and understandings but beyond those difference we still have one thing in common; we are all human beings with purposes. Whether you believe it or not everyone have at least one good purpose in their lives even those that do bad things.

Remember we do not have to accept what others do but we should at least understand we all have choices and decisions. Let's begin today to be more enthused about making better decisions to be apart of the groups that are making progress in spreading the concept of making humanity great not just themselves and theirs.

So often the gender a person usually dictates the degree or level of a sincere connection and that group connection do sometimes discriminate towards opposite genders. Males tend to gravitate more to males and likewise females tend to relate with other females and both see each other as not only different but also the concept of alienating themselves from one another other than sexual intimacy and companionship. But not as two genders connecting and agreeing on specific agendas, which should be the key factors that connects us all as a human race not a gender bias race. But a race of humans connecting on the agendas of aspirations, sensibilities and a need to be loved despite our different body parts. When we then solidify we are humans first we will be able to unify with humane objectives.

7

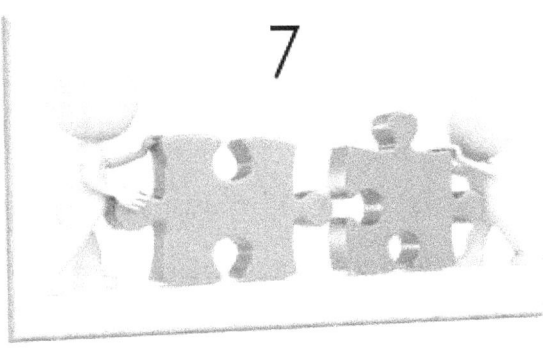

Unity Misconceived

There are many dangers of a group of people uniting, we must all examine the cause and perceptions of unifying or connecting before we actually be evolved in something that could be detrimental to others and ourselves. To be in unity only means to come or bring together for a common purpose or action and to form a unit, a bind and a group. We do not have to bond with certain groups. Be mindful of the connections and groups you associate yourselves to because while it is good to unify it could also be dangerous, with a negative connotation attached to the ideology of that particular organization. When we unify it should be to come together with respect for different ideas with the motive to help humanity as a whole in all aspect of human life.

We of many diverse groups with ideologies that detour others that are not a part of our group, is the wrong type of unifying and obviously has not worked or been successful in uniting us all as a human race. There are two types of unifying. The first type is to unify to conquer because of hate, and opposition which leads to a mindset of having to retaliate towards groups that oppose the ideology of that group. The other type of group is the one that has a compassionate heart and motive to unify for the sake and well being of all humanity. We must now consider our ways and secret thoughts and determine the real reason on why we as individuals choose to unite.

8

An Old African saying, "If you want to go somewhere fast go alone, if you want to go far go together."

Peace on Earth

The concept of each human obtaining peace in the world amongst all humans must come from having within each of our hearts and souls a sense and camaraderie amongst one another no matter the beliefs statue, ethnicity, social upbringing we all must adhere to possessing within our individual mindsets thoughts of good will towards one another, no matter what the circumstances are relative to certain conditions of the minds of each of us. Because none of us are perfect in all ultimate truths about all things it takes input from all humans in order to come to an appropriate and common understanding and concepts that will contribute to each of our positive personal growth and this world evolutionary advancements that will benefit all humans.

    The mission of this book is to prompt the awareness of the simplicity of eliminating social prejudices. This can only be initiated by you and I as an individual first, and then connect with others of like minds. You must begin to realize, after examining your ways, thoughts and secret motives of unifying, that you may have humbling thoughts and a conscious awareness of seeing things and your connections from a different and broader perspective and decide that in order to have peace within and in the world you have to change ranks or sides due to insight, revelation and love for the fellow human. To unify with others for the greater cause which is bigger and more profound than the positions of a single group that shun all others.

    We need to understand and come to the realization of that need to come together for the sake of all humanity as a whole in order for us all to prosper and be in good health. Being gratified with our decision to separate from the very things that promotes divisions. Just know you can develop a peace of mind knowing that it was, and it is okay to reject and deny the very concept of that group we were once affiliated with. Sometimes it takes us observing other groups doing wrong in order for it to be a catalyst to bring people together for the right motive, even more with a better understanding towards one another's broader outlook in reference to the fulfillment of humanity progression towards a better and more peaceful future.

About the Author

Carter M. Head is a life coach, a minister, and is one of the most dynamic, realistic, and sought-out conference speakers. Carter is a graduate of Andersonville Theological Seminary and Alumni of West Georgia College. Carter founded and established many outreach organizations in reference to feeding and clothing the indigent. Carter also established the YL2 (Youth Leadership League of Henry County, GA), and he coproduced three live stage plays emphasizing on the issues of our youth. Carter established the mentoring group called B.I.N.O. In addition, Carter is an author, grant writer, marriage counselor, and philanthropist.

Other Books by the Author

- ◊ Lying Mirrors
- ◊ Am I Trump?
- ◊ Questions with No Answers

www.ingramcontent.com/pod-product-compliance
Lightning Source LLC
Chambersburg PA
CBHW050447010526
44118CB00013B/1723